CENTURY SERIES FIGHTERS
F100 SUPER SABRE – F106 DELTA DART

CENTURY SERIES FIGHTERS

F100 SUPER SABRE – F106 DELTA DART

PETER R. FOSTER

Motorbooks International
Publishers & Wholesalers

For Maureen and All the patience

This USA edition published in 1992 by Motorbooks International,
Publishers & Wholesalers, PO Box 2, 729 Prospect Avenue,
Osceola, WI 54020, USA.

© Peter R. Foster 1992
Published by Airlife Publishing Ltd., Shrewsbury, England, 1992

Printed and bound in Singapore by Kyodo Printing Co. (S'pore) Pte Ltd

The information in this book is true and complete to the best of our knowledge. All recommendations
are made without any guarantee on the part of the author or publisher, who also disclaim any liability
incurred in connection with the use of this data or specific details.

We recognize that some words, model names and designations, for example,
mentioned herein are the property of the trademark holder. We use them for
identification purposes only. This is not an official publication.

Library of Congress Cataloging-in-Publication Data
ISBN 0-87938-667-3

Motorbooks International books are also available at discounts in bulk quantity for industrial or
sales-promotional use. For details write to Special Sales Manager at the Publisher's address.

INTRODUCTION

Although second generation jet fighters, the Century Series were the first aircraft to benefit from all available jet technology. Most of them did not see glory in combat, but this did not prevent them from fulfilling their role as peacekeepers in the skies of the free world.

Most designs appeared at a time of relative world peace which only the Cold War threatened, and there were several periods in which esprit de corps outweighed tactical thinking in the design schools, with results that have captured the imagination of aviator and enthusiast alike. This book is a tribute to those thrilling designs.

Acknowledgements are due to all the air arms concerned and to the help and advice of all those who have contributed to make this portfolio possible. I would particularly like to thank Robbie Shaw, Don Spering, Don Jay, Hans Schröder and H. J. van Broekshuizen for the use of their material.

Peter R. Foster
Brampton

Below: Once the backbone of NATO, the F-104 is the last operational Century Series fighter and one that epitomises the designs of Kelly Johnson.

Opposite: The North American F-100 Super Sabre or 'Hun' as it came to be known was the backbone of the United States' tactical jet air power before the advent of the F-4 Phantom, totalling some 16 wings by mid-1957. The Hun was also the first major jet type to see action in South East Asia, both with the regular airforce and air national guard units. The first such ANG unit to re-equip with the type was the 188TFS New Mexico ANG which began receiving the F-100A version of the aircraft in 1958.

The unit was to have a long association with the Hun until converting to the LTV A-7D Corsair in 1975, when its Super Sabres were distributed amongst other guard units. However the F-100C models were retired to Davis Monthan in the early seventies, many still retaining the grey colour scheme and unit markings as depicted in this photograph.

(Peter R. Foster)

Below: Prior to the war in South East Asia many aircraft operated in a natural metal finish although exotic unit markings were abundant. However Vietnam soon altered this and a camouflage scheme was adopted. This became generally known as South East Asia colours. One or two aircraft avoided camouflage colours, which in the case of the Hun was no doubt eased by its timely withdrawal from the area. Here F-100F 56-3944 in natural metal can be seen operating with the 152TFTS Arizona ANG. *(Peter R. Foster)*

Opposite: Inflight refuelling capability on the Hun did not come about until the advent of the F-100D/F models, when it was the drogue and probe method that was adopted — something not to find favour with later USAF types. Seen head on, the Hun clearly shows its supersonic lines while the probe on the starboard wing is clearly a design afterthought. *(Peter R. Foster)*

Below: Apart from the F-104 Starfighter, 'Century Series' USAF fighters saw only limited operation with other users. Those countries which were selected to receive what was then relatively sophisticated hardware did so under the Mutual Defence Aid Plan (MDAP). This meant that although operated by the country concerned the funding had come through Congress and the aircraft were therefore effectively still US property.

Three members of NATO were to use the F-100, France, Turkey and Denmark. Of these Denmark received only 49 'D' and 11 'F' models for operation by Esk727 and 730 at Skrydstrup. Here 55-2779 is seen in 1969, still resplendent in a non-camouflage scheme.

Opposite: The F-100 last saw front line service with the 48th TFW at Lakenheath, Suffolk. However South East Asia was to be its proving ground and along with many other types it entered the fray in its peacetime schemes. Here at Da Nang in April 1966 an F-100D of 416TFS, still in natural metal, is serviced prior to its next mission. *(via Robert Dorr)*

Below: France equipped one wing with the F-100D/F — at Toul-Rosieres — and retained the type until transition to the Sepecat Jaguar in 1976. Once again the aircraft retained the natural metal scheme until late in their operational lives when camouflage was adopted. With their demise in France the United States exercised its option to have the redundant airframes returned for disposal. This was undertaken at RAF Sculthorpe where this photograph of 42146 in the markings of EC2/11 was taken.

This particular aircraft escaped camouflaging having seen its last years in storage with EAA601 at Chateaudun. Not all of the F-100s supplied to France were subject to MDAP funding, therefore only certain designated airframes were returned. This totalled 25 'D' and four 'F' models most of which found secure homes.

Opposite: Turkey was the final NATO member to use the Super Sabre and did so at 3ciAHU Konya until quite recently. It was also the only other user of the 'C' model, which along with 'D's and 'F's totalled a reported figure of around 300 aeroplanes. Here F-100C 41826 is seen on a rare visit to Germany in 1973.

Below: Denmark along with most other users of the 'Hun' camouflaged its aircraft. Nobody ever said that the aircraft was a particularly easy aeroplane to fly. To this end the Danish Air Force was to lose some 31 aircraft. To maintain a viable force during 1975 it purchased outright from the United States 14 F-100F twin seat aircraft, 12 of which were to survive until de-activation in favour of the F-16 in 1983.

Like France, Denmark returned its MDAP aircraft to USAF charge at RAF Sculthorpe. However in this case the 23 aircraft concerned were immediately transferred to Turkey to continue in service for a further five years. Here F-100D G769 in the familiar Danish camouflage scheme is seen prior to its transfer to Turkey on 6 November 1981. *(K. Rowt)*

Opposite: The final export of the F-100 was to Nationalist China who are believed to be still operating the type today. The country received approximately 90 F-100A/D/F models which were latterly used with the Air Force Reserve units. Preserved in Tapai at Chung Cheng Aviation Museum is F-100A 31550. *(Andy Heape)*

Below: The remaining Danish twin seat F-100F's soldiered on until 1983, when six were sold to Flight Systems Inc for target facilities work. The remainder found their way into ground roles in Denmark itself. Here 56-3927 is seen on final approach to RAF Alconbury on 17 October 1979 and although belonging to Esk730 sports a No. 315 Squadron/Klu badge on the fin. *(Peter R. Foster)*

Opposite: The Air National Guard began receiving the F-100A model in 1958 and, following their withdrawal from South East Asia and Europe, many units upgraded to the 'D' variant. The 118TFS Connecticut at Bradley Field, Windsor Locks was one of these units and was to retain the 'Hun' until receiving the Fairchild A-10A in 1979. The unit was also one of the few ANG units to abide by 'TAC' policy in tail coding its aircraft as can be seen in this shot of 55-3665. *(Don Spering/AIR)*

Below: 162TFTS Arizona ANG was the F-100 ANG Training unit and holds the same role today for the GD F-16 Fighting Falcon. Operating from Tucson's International Airport the fighters are intermixed with civilian traffic of all kinds whilst the fine flying weather offered in Arizona makes the location an ideal choice for such a unit. F-100D 56-2993 is seen here parked outside some of the new facilities built for introduction of the A-7. Beneath the lower fuselage can be seen the large air brake, a characteristic of the F-100 series. *(Peter R. Foster)*

Opposite: Clearly visible in this climb-out shot of 56-3028 are the leading edge slats which helped to give the aircraft improved handling characteristics. This aircraft is from the 163rd TFS Indiana ANG at Fort Wayne and was on deployment to Europe when this photograph was taken in 1976. *(Peter R. Foster)*

Overleaf: The Fairchild A-10A Thunderbolt II was to replace the 'Hun' with both Connecticut and Massachusetts Air National Guards. Here F-100F 56-3813/MA is seen in formation with a pair of A-10s, 78-0612/18, during the final phase of transition in August 1979. The refuelling probe in the corner of the photograph reveals that the camera ship was another 'Hun'. *(Don Spering/AIR)*

Below: France retained approximately 20 F-100s for service with EC4/11 'Jura' in Djibouti. These aircraft remained operational until 1978 when they were replaced with the Mirage IIIC. For the next ten years the aircraft were to remain on the airfield as decoys but several examples have now been brought back to France for display purposes, four of which are at Savigny les Beaune. Here F-100D 42125 complete with shark's mouth markings is seen in Djibouti in May 1981, this is believed to be one of the examples that has returned to France.

Opposite: Although belonging to the 128TFS Georgia ANG, F-100D 56-3093, shows signs of a previous owner. The word 'one' can be clearly seen on the reheat area, signifying its use by the USAF Aerobatic display team 'The Thunderbirds'. The USAF's most prestigious unit was to operate both the 'C' and 'D' variants of the 'Hun' although it had converted from the F-100C to the F-105B in 1964 only to return to the F-100D after five displays in the 'Thud'.
(Peter R. Foster)

Below: Tracor/Flight Systems still retain the former Danish AF F-100Fs in the role of target facilities under contract to the United States' Air Force. Three of these aircraft are regularly employed operating from Decimomannu in Sardinia. At the company's main base in Mojave, California, further examples are employed as system test vehicles. *(Bob Archer)*

Opposite: Flight Systems are also under contract to convert the vast store of surplus F-100s to target drone vehicles for use at the White Sands missile test range and the ACMI range at Tyndall AFB. These aircraft are returned to an airworthy state by the Mojave technicians and then flown to either Tyndall or Holloman AFBs to be used either as manned targets or radio-controlled drones. F-100D 56-3017 bearing the conversion number 186 is one of around thirty normally to be found at either location. *(Peter R. Foster)*

Below: Taxiing in at Tyndall QF-100D 56-3048 returns after a target facilities sortie during the 1982 'William Tell' weapons competition. The '094' on the reheat area signifies the 94th example to be converted to drone configuration. At the demise of the 'Hun' from service the USAF had a store of nearly 400 suitable airframes for this cost-effective operation, the bulk of which have been converted. (Peter R. Foster)

Opposite: Each QF-100D converted is considered airworthy for up to ten target sorties. After that they are declared live targets and are invariably destroyed during live firing tests. However as missiles are designed to explode in close proximity to the target these aircraft are often recovered from these types of sorties with effective battle damage and repaired by the unit for further flights. Every flight after the initial ten is considered a bonus over the project costs. (Peter R. Foster)

Below: With the supply of surplus F-100 airframes within the United Stares nearing its end Tracor/Flight Systems have begun to evaluate the many surplus airframes in open store in Turkey. This evaluation began in July 1989 with the delivery of an F-100C/D and F variant back to their Mojave base from Konya in Turkey. The flight was beset with many problems not least the effects of open storage on the airframes. The aircraft transitted through Stansted Airport in England on 4 August 1989 but on 4 September the F-100C depicted here, still displaying its Turkish unit markings, was still at Goose Bay with Technical problems. It is understood that in excess of fifty airframes are available to be returned for conversion which will presumably include the former Danish aircraft. However, following the experiences of the initial three it is thought the remainder will be dismantled and returned by sea.
(Peter R. Foster)

Opposite: The glory of natural metal and high visibility marks survived late with the Voodoo, partly because of its air defence role and partly because of Aerospace Defence Command policy. Here in 1966 is F-101B 80310 from the 29FIS at Malmstrom AFB.
(Robert F. Dorr)

Below: The Voodoo powered by two J-57 engines was very quick and as such achieved during 'Operation Sun Run' on 27 November 1957 the remarkable record of flying between Los Angeles and New York at an average speed of 781.74mph. There were three 'Sun Run' Voodoos but it was No. 3, RF-101C 60165 flown by Lt Gus Klatt that achieved the record.

Opposite: The Voodoo saw very limited service outside the United States with only the 81st TFW in England receiving the type. It was here that the first 50 production F-101A fighters were based. *(Robert F. Dorr)*

Opposite: The final two operators with ADC were 136FIS New York ANG and 111FIS Texas ANG. Both units converted to the F-4 Phantom, but up to the early eighties F-101's continued to play an important role in the policing of the skies around the US coast. Here 70317 of 111FIS is seen rotating from Tyndall AFB during the 'William Tell' weapons meet in 1980 whilst the Phantom departing in the opposite direction belongs to the recently converted 178FIS. *(Peter R. Foster)*

Below: It was the F-101B version of the Voodoo that was to survive the longest, remaining in service up until 1984. The aircraft was designed to meet the threat of the manned bomber. The prime operator was to be Aerospace Defence Command with whom an eventual 17 Squadrons were to convert to the type. It was however the ADC units of the air national guard that were to be the last users. Here sporting their familiar slogan 'Happy Hooligans' is 57-0250 of 178FIS North Dakota ANG. *(Peter R. Foster)*

Below: 123FIS Oregon ANG located in Portland provided the ADC cover for the north western part of the United States, a role it shared with the Delta Darts of the 318th FIS at McChord AFB. The natural metal finish had given way to a grey scheme in the sixties but this did not have any adverse effect on unit markings. In this photograph an Oregon Voodoo is pictured outside the 'Alert' facility.

Opposite: Tyndall, although best known as the venue of the 'William Tell' fighter weapons meet was also home to the ADC training units. In latter years the Air Defence Weapons Centre housed three squadrons including 2 FITS on the Voodoo. The unit had responsibility for training all '101' pilots and WSOs on aircraft type and weapon delivery. Here with chute streaming an F-101F twin sticker comes to a halt on one of Tyndall's parallel runways. *(Peter R. Foster)*

Below: Florida and the Gulf of Mexico are very suitable for aircrew training, with very few sorties being lost to weather conditions. It is true that the Hurricane season can cause problems but these events are minimal. Here high over the Everglades in close formation is an F-101B of 2FITS. *(via Don Jay)*

Opposite: In 1961 Canada took delivery of 66 F-101B/F Voodoos to replace the aging CF-100 Interceptors. Later in the early seventies as the USAF began to phase out the type from regular units a further 66 were extensively modernised and these were exchanged for the original aircraft. Some of those returning to USAF charge were in turn modified to RF-101H standard and assigned to the 192nd TRS Nevada ANG at Reno. Looking down from the Reno tower 13 'Recce' Voodoos together with two F-101F twin stickers can be seen. *(Peter R. Foster)*

Below: The penultimate 'William Tell' meet was the last to have Voodoos in any significant numbers. Here climbing out is a 2FITS F-101F fitted with a 'hot pod'. Apart from aircrew training the ADWC was responsible for teaching the art of air intercept and missile firing. The instructors therefore flew target sorties, some of which included a variety of electronic gadgetry. *(Peter R. Foster)*

Opposite: New York Voodoos lasted right to the end although their attractive markings were to disappear with ADC being absorbed by TAC. Here on their ramp at Niagara Falls in 1976 is F-101B 80262 being prepared for the next sortie. *(Peter R. Foster)*

Below: With second generation fighters primarily having a hard light rather than staged afterburner, the problem of overspeed in cold conditions was ever present. It was conceivable for the speed on a take off run to exceed the permitted tolerance of the nose wheel retraction. This was one of the problems for which Voodoo pilots had to watch. Here 111FIS F-101B 80276 begins to rotate. *(Peter R. Foster)*

Opposite: With TAC exerting influence over former ADC units the toning down of markings was not long in coming about. At the penultimate 'William Tell' meet it was clear that the change of command was beginning to have effect. The 136FIS F-101B depicted here has a much-reduced marking scheme although other striking attributes began to appear such as the 'I love NY' marking on the inside of the intake. *(Peter R. Foster)*

Below: The main air defence armament of the Voodoo was the Falcon AAM, three of which could be carried in a rotary weapons bay. However, apart from this and the MG-13 fire control system the 'B' version also had two external hardpoints as seen on this shot to accommodate a pair of AIR-2 Genie AAMs with nuclear warheads. *(Peter R. Foster)*

Opposite: 58 of Canada's original Voodoos were returned to USAF charge with those not receiving conversion to RF-101H standard eventually meeting the smelter's torch at Davis Monthan. The second batch maintained Canada's NORAD contribution until 1985 when the final aircraft were phased out. Seen over the frozen Sagueny River this Voodoo blends well with its background. *(Peter R. Foster)*

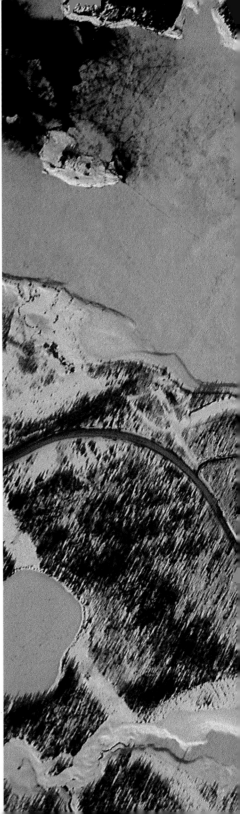

Below: Towards the end of Voodoo operations in Canada the three surviving squadrons each painted one aircraft in special marks. At Bagotville No. 425 Squadron created a red and blue 'Alouette' to depict their name. At Comox No. 409 Squadron created 'Hawk One' after their name of Night Hawks and at Chatham 416 created this very attractive scheme on 101043. *(Robbie Shaw)*

Opposite: This Canadian CF-101B from 425 Squadron taxies in from a sortie in the final year of Voodoo operations at Tyndall. In 1982 the Canadians sent a joint team from both 425 and 409 Squadrons. *(Peter R. Foster)*

Below: A few CF-101s retained the silver scheme until the end. Here seen at Tyndall is CF-101F 101031 marked with the 'Lynx's Head' of 416 Squadron from CFB Chatham. This unit was the last fighter unit to operate the Voodoo, standing down at the end of 1984. *(Peter R. Foster)*

Opposite: Clean lines and long legs made the Voodoo an ideal interceptor. However policing the eastern seaboard on what was known as 'Cold Shaft' necessitated deploying to Gander and intercepting the trade at extreme range which without an inflight refuelling capability could prove disastrous for the crews involved. *(Peter R. Foster)*

Below: The small wing on the Voodoo made it an easy aeroplane to formate close to. Such a wing did create problems with the AOA but an experienced operator could live on the edge of the envelope without any undue worry. *(Peter R. Foster)*

Opposite: Peeling away to start 'PI's these three Voodoos blend well into the frozen wastes of Quebec Province. Even against blue skies the grey colour scheme was hard to detect. However in the world of air defence it was the skill of the radar operator more than the naked eye that gleaned the kill. *(Peter R. Foster)*

Below: The final Voodoo to operate anywhere in the world was in Canadian markings but the property of the US Government. To provide a realistic ECM threat in the air defence theatre, Canada chose to have the loan of a former ADWC F-101B complete with hot pod attachment. The aircraft, 80300, upon retirement from Tyndall was passed onto No. 414 Squadron/CAF at CFB North Bay and given the serial 101067 following on directly from the 66 fighter aircraft. *(Peter R. Foster)*

Opposite: Known as the 'electric Voodoo' the two J-57 engines provided greater power than the CC117 Falcon 20s then in use as ECM trainers. As such more forceful jamming could be created, giving the crews a greater threat to deal with. Unfortunately the life span of this jet was severely limited — its eventual demise coming in 1986 when it was returned to USAF charge. *(Peter R. Foster)*

Below: Canada was not the only non-US user of the Voodoo. Nationalist China received between six and nine RF-101s in 1959. It was these jets that most likely saw the Voodoo complete its first combat missions. The Nationalists were able to photograph strips of mainland China up to 100 miles inland and this went on until China gained faster fighters and surface to air missiles. The jets were eventually retired through operational attrition of one kind or another with the only known surviving example being 41505 which is displayed at Chung Cheng Aviation Museum in Tapai. *(Andy Heape)*

Opposite: With air brakes just beginning to extend this Voodoo makes a hard break to port over the bleak Canadian terrain. *(Peter R. Foster)*

Below: Equally unique is the sole civilian Voodoo. F-101B 70410 registered as N8234 to the University of Colorado for weather research. The aircraft operated for many years in this role from Buckley ANGB sporting a long barber's pole and named 'The Grey Ghost'. This shot was taken in June 1974 and the jet was still present a year later. *(Don Jay)*

Opposite: The 'Duce' or F-102 suffered more early problems than the rest of the Century fighters. It was the third to use the hard light J-57 engine and was perhaps ultimately the most used of all the fighters. The F-102 went on to see service in all US theatres of operation and served with 46 regular USAF units and 20 ANG units. Here fitted with an inflight refuelling probe is 61352. *(Robert F. Dorr)*

Below: California was one of the late users of the F-102, trading it in for the Cessna O-2A in 1975 — not a popular move with the crews. The unit operated from Ontario Airport as the 196FIS and passed its aircraft into storage at Davis Monthan. *(Don Jay)*

Opposite: The Duce was the first of the Century Series to retire from active service. The Guard also began disposing of its aircraft quite early with the final units standing down in 1975. Here in the colours of the Vermont ANG is 70855. The shot was taken in 1971 shortly before the unit converted to the EB-57B Canberra. *(Don Jay)*

Below: Perhaps the final user of the Duce was the 199FIS at Hickam AFB Hawaii. They converted to the F-4C in 1976. The aircraft employed an all-missile system carried internally in a weapons bay in the belly. The primary weapon was the AIM-4A radar guided AAM and AIM-4C infra-red guided AAM, six of which could be carried. *(Don Jay)*

Opposite: In 1973 the Sperry Corporation was awarded a contract to convert 215 F-102 Delta Daggers into remote-controlled target drones. The bulk of these airframes were stored at Davis Monthan and following de-preserving were ferried to the Sperry facility at Crestview, Florida. Here seen at Holloman AFB, New Mexico, are a trio of PQM-102s two of which retain their former marks with a high-vis red tail. The middle jet, 61400, is painted in the Sperry house colours. *(Peter R. Foster)*

Below: The decision to replace the Firebee sub-scale drones with life-size ones was partly taken out of a need to know how to dispose of the surplus aircraft of the 6,000 or so then in storage following the end of America's involvement in the Vietnam war. Equally it was considered that 'Duce' possessed a marked resemblance in silhouette to the 'enemy' Su-19, Mig-23 and Mig-25 fighters. 61223, conversion 748, still retains its camouflage from previous service with the 194FIS at Fresno. *(Peter R. Foster)*

Opposite: Most, if not all, of the F-102s converted to drone configuration were eventually shot down in the Gulf of Mexico or over the White Sands missile range in New Mexico. 61254 is shown here over the drone field at Tyndall AFB in October 1982. *(Don Jay)*

Below: Export of the 'Duce' was limited to two NATO countries. Greece received enough aircraft to equip 342 Moira at Tanagra and these remained in service until replaced by the Mirage F1CG. At that time the surviving 20 aircraft were relegated to ground duties, most of them still survive today.

Opposite: QF-102A 61443 comes to a halt at Tyndall in October 1982. The conversion of these aircraft moved to Litchfield Park, Arizona from 1978 onwards until the programme was complete. *(Peter R. Foster)*

Below: Turkey received the 'Duce' on a par with Greece to maintain the balance between the two countries. They however equipped two units, 142 Filo at Murted and 182 Filo at Merzifon. Here at Yesilkoy is F-102A 0-53386. *(Robbie Shaw)*

Opposite: USAF use of the Starfighter was very limited. Adopted solely for ADC units Lockheed had received a contract for 155 aircraft in 1955 and operational acceptance was achieved in January 1958. However ADC disposed of its aircraft in 1959, turning them over to the air national guard. By the early seventies the only F-104s to be found operating in the USA were those of the 4510CCTW at Luke AFB. The aircraft at Luke were the property of the German Air Force but were wholly maintained by Lockheed. The operation to train German crews was to last some twenty years and when this finally ceased in 1982 the bulk of the aircraft were sold to Nationalist China. *(Peter R. Foster)*

Below: The last Air National Guard unit to operate the Starfighter was the 198thTFS in Puerto Rico. These F-104C model aircraft continued in service until 1975 when the type was withdrawn in favour of the LTV A-7D Corsair. *(G. B. Rhodes)*

Opposite: Of all the Century Series fighters the Starfighter was the most widely used. With licence production in six countries an amazing 2581 aircraft were produced. TF-104G 63-8457 seen turning off the runway with the Arizona mountains in the background. This Starfighter was, like all twin seat versions, a product of the Lockheed production line. *(Peter R. Foster)*

Below: Lockheed were responsible for the building of all twin seat aircraft. 2802 in the markings of WS10 at Jever bore the c/n 5932 confirming its parentage. Germany, realising that the Starfighter was a good multi-role aeroplane and one that could help rebuild their aerospace industry, signed their contract to licence build the F-104 in March 1959. *(Peter R. Foster)*

Opposite: In all, Germany went on to equip thirteen units with a total of 700 airframes including both air force and navy geschwader. F-104Gs 2122 and 2124 from MFG-2 depicted here were Fiat-built recce aircraft and served with the unit until its transition to Tornados in 1987. *(Hans J. Schroder)*

Below: The splinter camouflage adopted by the German air force was retained for the bulk of the aircraft's career, and as can be seen in this shot of 2233 it blends well with European terrain. *(Hans J. Schroder)*

Opposite: Following Germany's lead Canada signed contracts to produce 200 airframes for its own forces in September 1959. The CF-104s were basically similar to the standard F-104G with some internal differences. This aircraft seen over the Bavarian countryside is fitted with a practice bomb dispenser on the centre line station. *(Peter R. Foster)*

Below: Canadian aircraft served primarily in Europe with the No. 1 Air Division comprising No. 1 Wing at Marville, France, No. 3 Wing at Zweibrucken and No. 4 Wing at Sollingen. The remaining aircraft were assigned to No. 6 OTU at CFB Cold Lake. *(Peter R. Foster)*

Opposite: The F-104's small wing created steady handling characteristics and therefore made close formation easy. These three aircraft are from No. 439 Squadron at Baden-Sollingen. *(Peter R. Foster)*

Below: Japan was the third customer to sign a production contract for the Starfighter, doing so in January 1960. The production run covered 190 airframes built by Mitsubishi heavy industries. On top of this they also reassembled 20 knock-down F-104J aircraft from the Lockheed line together with the 20 F-104DJ twin seats. *(Peter R. Foster)*

Opposite: JASDF operated the venerable Starfighter from April 1962 until the last examples were retired from the Air Proving Wing at Gifu in the mid 1980s. For the bulk of their career the aircraft operated in an all-metal scheme similar to this 206 Hikotai aircraft. This unit used the Starfighter between 1966 and 1978. The blue marking on the tail is a stylized '7' for '7th Kokudan' which is located at Hyakuri AB near the city of Mito — famous for its Japanese-style plum garden. The plum flower can be seen imposed on the foreground of the figure seven. *(Peter R. Foster)*

Below: The Koninklijke Luchtmacht or Netherlands Air Force began procurement of the Starfighter in April 1960. The aircraft came from both the Fokker and Fiat production lines and were operated by five squadrons from Leeuwarden and Volkel air bases. D-8062 pictured here landing at Volkel in June 1983 was the last front line unit to operate the type and converted to the F-16 later that year. *(Peter R. Foster)*

Opposite: Nyutabaru AB was home to 202 Hikotai as the Starfighter training unit between 1976 and 1982. Unlike Europe where everything now operates from hardened accommodation Japanese units all operate off a flightline with a large amount of hangar space being required. The yellow and red 'V' marking on this particular aircraft is a stylized roman five for '5th Kokudan' to which 202 Hikotai belonged. *(Peter R. Foster)*

Below: The other Belgian wing to operate the F-104 was No. 10 Wing at Kleine Brogel. The two squadrons assigned here were nos. 23 and 31 smaldeel, which maintained Belgium's strike capability. FX61 seen here is landing at RAF Waddington during a NATO air defence exercise and clearly shows the Starfighter's low approach. *(Peter R. Foster)*

Opposite: FX-67 is seen here displaying the badge of No. 1 Wing from Beauvechain on its fin and the marking of No. 350 smaldeel on the intake. This unit was part of the Belgian air defence wing and operated the type between 1963 and 1980. Many of the Starfighters built in Europe were subject to MAP funding and as such were passed onto other users upon their retirement. *(Peter R. Foster)*

Below: Italy was the last member of the European consortium to sign production contracts for the Starfighter. Aircraft built by FIAT at Turin were incorporated in Dutch and German inventories whilst the company went on to develop the Super Starfighter. Known as the F-104S the aircraft incorporated a number of significant changes including a mid-altitude BVR capability. Shown here is an 'S' model belonging to Italy's 'Tiger' squadron, 21°Gruppo 53°Stormo which is armed with both AIM-7F Sparrow and AIM-9P AAMs. *(G. Candiani)*

Opposite: Apart from building 200 CF-104s for its own armed forces Canadair also produced a number of F-104Gs for the United States. These aircraft were then distributed to Norway, Turkey, Greece, Spain and Nationalist China. 64-17763/4337 depicted here is one of these aircraft and is in the markings of the Chinese Nationalist Air Force. The island of Taiwan is today a haven for the F-104 with surplus German, Danish and Japanese examples having been transferred there in the absence of more sophisticated hardware. *(Don Jay)*

Below: The remaining Italian Starfighter units are now re-equipping with the F-104ASA, an 'S' model with a mid-life update. Also the large unit codes as depicted on MM6778/4-7 here have largely disappeared in favour of smaller ones. This particular aircraft is seen at Twenthe in Holland whilst on exchange with 315 Squadron/Klu. It still bears the red and white checkers of No. 56 Squadron/RAF with whom it visited the previous year. *(Peter R. Foster)*

Opposite: The F-104S was used by Italy in both ground attack and air defence. Squadrons were tasked with a primary role in one of these areas and each wing had one squadron dedicated to each role. Here MM6705 the fifth production 'S' is seen in the markings of 23°Gruppo 5°Stormo which was primarily an air defence unit. Its sister squadron, 102°Gruppo, specialized in ground attack. *(Peter R. Foster)*

Below: Denmark lost ten of its original F-104s to accidents. In September 1971 the Government, realising that attrition would soon reduce the air defence capability to one squadron, purchased outright from Canada 21 surplus aircraft. They then took the unprecedented action of converting them all to F-104G standard. It was however to be the original MAP aircraft that were to stay in service until the retirement of the type in April 1986. R-342 depicted here clearly shows the AIM-9 AAM rails on the centreline station permitting the tip tanks to be retained for increased endurance. *(Peter R. Foster)*

Opposite: Caught over the murky skies of the north German plains, MM6873 from 36°Stormo, looks on as an RAF Phantom from No. 92 Squadron closes alongside. *(Peter R. Foster)*

Below: The lizard marking scheme has been applied to the entire air force Tornado fleet and RF-4E Phantoms. The Starfighter was by this time well on its way to retirement. JBG-34 from Memmingham was the final front line unit and therefore ended up with all the low time aircraft which included those recently overhauled. Here 2064, a Lockheed-built aircraft and 2652, one of the last built for the air force by Messerschmitt formate on a sortie out of Memmingham in May 1987. *(Hans J. Schroder)*

Opposite: Germany initially began replacing its Starfighters with the F-4 Phantom in 1971. At that time the two Recce units of AKG-51 and 52 began receiving the RF-4E. Next came the dedicated air defence units of JG-71 and 74 who received the F-4F finally to be followed by one ground attack unit, JBG-36 in 1973. The remaining 'mud movers' continued until the introduction of the Tornado. The four aircraft from JBG-34 depicted here in late 1984 are mainly in the original splinter camouflage scheme although one example had by this time received the new 'lizard' colours. *(Hans J. Schroder)*

Below: Prior to JBG-34 converting to the Tornado it was the turn of MFG-2 from Eggebeck in the Flensberg Peninsula. Here TF-104G 2825 makes a low approach to its parent airfield in November 1981.
(Peter R. Foster)

Opposite: RAF Cottesmore, as home to the Tri-national Tornado Training Establishment, played host to many visiting Starfighters whilst the respective units were converting to the Tornado. Seen on approach is a further lizard example from JBG-34 in the shape of 2644 which was one of the few '104's still flying in Germany in the 1990's. *(Peter R. Foster)*

Below: Wehrtechnische Dientstelle 61, or WTD-61 as it is better known, is the German Air Force test unit at Manching. The unit is responsible for both aircraft and weapon technology studies and as such maintain a selection of aircraft types on strength. This included around ten Starfighters which were used for weapon trials and photo chase duties. Included in these is 2008 the eighth production 'G' model from the Lockheed line which is seen here landing at Fairford with the imposing shape of a B-52G in the background. *(Peter R. Foster)*

Opposite: Echelon starboard 'Go'. As a sign of the times this four-ship of Memmingham Starfighters has reversed the balance in colour trend from the previous shot. The aircraft, 2630, 2645, 2064 and 2652 remained with the unit until deactivation in type and are all now believed to reside in store at Erding. *(Hans J. Schroder)*

Below: Turkey originally received a small batch of Canadair and Lockheed-built Starfighters under MAP. Since then it has received large quantities of surplus aircraft from Belgium, Holland, Norway, Canada and Germany. These have equipped units with the 4th, 6th, 8th and 9th Tactical air forces at Murted, Bandirma, Balikesir and Diyarbakir. Most of these aircraft have retained their original camouflage schemes but those that have been repainted have adopted the German splinter scheme. Here former German TF-104G 2739 is seen marked as 6-741 adopting the c/n for a serial prefixed by the air force code whilst operating with 162 Filo. *(Peter R. Foster)*

Opposite: Canada passed 50 CF-104s onto Turkey for use with the 8th Tactical Air Force at Diyarbakir, many of which were overhauled prior to delivery. The three aircraft depicted here, 104770/841/845 were all amongst the aircraft given as a 'gift' to the Turkish government. Gracefully gliding through the cloud tops, the F-104 was small and agile enough to be a real threat to any enemy force. The jet, having very small, thin wings was rock steady and could operate down in the weeds with near impunity, delivering its ordnance with reasonable accuracy. *(Peter R. Foster)*

Below: Although the final military use of the Starfighter in the United States ceased operations in 1975, NASA at Edwards AFB has retained a selection of modified F-104A/B/N and TF-104G aircraft on strength as high speed chase vehicles since the type's conception. Seen in the NASA hangar at Edwards AFB is former F-104B 57-1303/N819NA. This aircraft has since been retired and is now preserved at McClellen AFB. *(Peter R. Foster)*

Opposite: JASDF F-104J of the Air Proving Wing at Gifu seen head-on shows the sleek pleasing lines of the Starfighter which gained it the attribute of 'missile with a man in it'.

Below: N811NA is an F-104N used both as a high speed chase and as as astronaut training vehicle. This aircraft is reported to have the Lockheed c/n 683C-4045. The surplus air force F-104A and B models found their way into service with Pakistan, Nationalist China and Jordan, all of whom are believed to have used the aircraft in action. *(Peter R. Foster)*

Opposite: 'Pins Out' last chance check and thumbs up clearance to taxi. 3°Stormo intends to replace its RF-104Gs with the AMX during 1991. Here MM6563/3-43 is seen at RAF Marham for the 1989 exchange with No. 27 Squadron. *(Peter R. Foster)*

Below: Turkey's receipt of 40 Aeritalia built F-104S aircraft to equip 142 and 182 Filo at Murted occurred in 1978. Attrition with these aircraft has been high and the air defence role is believed to have passed to the General Dynamics F-16Cs now coming on line.

Opposite: Climbing away with reheat fully on the F-104G with four external tanks in a Hi-Lo-Hi profile has an endurance in excess of two hours. In spite of being a second generation jet it is still a very impressive performer.
(Peter R. Foster)

Below: Most test and experimental establishments use types long after their demise from front line service. These aircraft serve in a variety of roles from system test aircraft to photo chase. They serve the longest in the last category, as when new types are being tested the only items of equal performance are invariably those of the previous generation. 104704 seen here retained its natural metal scheme until withdrawn from service, spending its entire career with AETE at CFB Cold Lake. *(CAF)*

Opposite: The last Starfighters to fly with the Canadian Armed Forces were a pair of CF-104s belonging to AETE at Cold Lake. Here marked with the unit's distinctive red cross is 104646 acting as chase to the new CF-18. *(CAF)*

Below: The 'Thud' as it became known was the mainstay of the USAF' tactical bombing campaign in South East Asia. The type survived until attrition had reduced numbers to such an extent that it was not a viable option to maintain it within the theatre of operations. However with the electronic war increasing on an impressive scale it was here that a new concept was to see its retention in the 'Wild Weasel' capacity. Much of the development of these operations was carried out by the 57FWW at Nellis AFB. Therefore the 66FWS was to have a mixture of F-105D/F/G aircraft on strength up until 1975. Here we see a pair of aircraft at Nellis in the spring of 1974.
(Peter R. Foster)

Opposite: The Republic F-105 Thunderchief became somewhat of a political pawn in the game of deterrent played by the armed forces. When the shift to nuclear capability was at its highest TAC saw the Thunderchief as a saviour as it was an aeroplane that looked and handled like a fighter but had a bomb bay bigger than a B-17, and could carry nuclear weapons. However, although this guaranteed the type's survival it was as a conventional fighter bomber that it was to claim fame and create its own place in history. Here in a typical South East Asia scheme is an F-105G.
(Peter R. Foster)

Opposite: The F-105B variant of the 'Thud' was a relatively small procurement with only three front line squadrons equipping with the type. When the 'D' came along these aircraft were then passed onto the Air National Guard at McGuire AFB and to the Air Force Reserve at Hill AFB, Ogden, Utah. Seen against the splendid backdrop of the Rockies, 57-5838 served with the 466thTFS until supplanted by the 'D' in the early eighties. *(Peter R. Foster)*

Below: Following the withdrawal from South East Asia the modified F-105G 'Wild Weasel' aircraft were assigned to the 561stTFS under the 35thTFW at George AFB in California. These aircraft were to remain in the front line inventory for another four years when the type finally left the service of TAC — a role it had maintained since May 1958, over twenty years previously. This shot shows a trio of 'Weasel' aircraft at George AFB in April 1974. *(Peter R. Foster)*

Below: Upon reassignment from South East Asia the surviving F-105D models were to be found with a number of AFRES and ANG units. Here at Tinker AFB, Oke, the 465thTFS formed part of the 301stTFW along with the 'B's at Hill and the 457thTFS at Carswell. The tailcode 'SH' was introduced on the aircraft in 1975, the unit having used 'UC' up until that time. *(Peter R. Foster)*

Opposite: The 'B' model of the Thud joined the New Jersey Air National Guard very early in its career. A pair of the unit's aircraft are seen here in formation with the States' other fighter unit 177FIG from Atlantic City with its F-106 Delta darts. *(Don Spering/AIR)*

Below: The Air National Guard received the bulk of the serving Thunderchiefs to equip four squadrons. Near to home the 121TFS at Andrews AFB as the District of Columbia ANG retained the type until 1981. In 1976 the unit was still very active with the type.
(Peter R. Foster)

Opposite: The 'Guard' F-105 units — TAC gains were very reluctant to follow TAC guidelines on the adoption of tail codes. All four units retained just the state name on their aircraft as depicted here on this trio of District of Columbia aircraft. This was, in 1981, to be short-lived as pressure was brought to bear for the guard to conform. However the F-105s, even the final ones, escaped altogether.
(Peter R. Foster)

Below: Apart from the deployment of Hill F-105s to Denmark, the other two AFRES units only visited Europe spasmodically in the latter years, whilst the Air Guard were even more noticeable by their absence. Here at their home base at Richard E. Byrd Field, Santon, Richmond, Virginia, the aircraft of the Virginia ANG saw out their days until the arrival of the LTV A-7D Corsair. *(Peter R. Foster)*

Opposite: Bombs gone, mission nearly over and a welcome top-up of fuel from the post-strike tankers stationed in relatively safe skies. It could so easily be Vietnam below this F-105D but in fact it is western England not far from Land's End and the aircraft is from the 466thTFS at Hill AFB en route to Denmark on a 'Coronet' deployment for exercise Oxbol during the summer of 1981. *(Robbie Shaw)*

Below: Most of the F-105s that survived had interesting histories. Most had also at some time in their careers received names and the art work that was an everyday part of life in SEA. At Richmond there was a Mst/Sgt Bailey who as a matter of course created an individual name for each and every one. The name 'Super Hog' comes from the nicknames applied to the Thunderchief. 'Thud' was perhaps the best known but 'Lead Sled', 'Ultra Hog', 'Thunderthud' and 'Chief' were others used. Also the 149thTFS at Richmond had converted to the F-105 from the F-84F which was known as the 'Hog', so perhaps 'Super Hog' was a compliment to its abilities. *(Peter R. Foster)*

Opposite: Fitted with the hard light J-75, which in an unreheated state still powers the TR-1, the Thud could create 26,000lbs of wet thrust. Fitted with a Doppler navigation system and the Thunderstick Fire Control System it could, in experienced hands, match anything the next generation of fighter bombers would produce. Perhaps this is another reason it survived so long. Here the distinctive shape of the intake can be seen as the lead aircraft breaks hard to starboard. *(Don Spering/AIR)*

Below: The Thunderchief began life with the reputation of being a difficult aircraft to fly. This was enhanced by the loss of a 'B' model with the Thunderbirds Aerial Display team, which ultimately saw the team reconvert to the F-100. However South East Asia more than altered this reputation to one of respect which lasted until the very end. The sound of the hard light of the J-75 is perhaps what will be missed by most, nostalgia for the remainder of the Thuds' attributes being reserved for that special breed of person capable of flying it. *(Don Spering/AIR)*

Opposite: A trio of fully camouflaged 'D's over the Great Salt Lake in Utah during 1983 — very much the twilight of the Thunderchiefs' career. The 466thTFS was to become the first part-time unit to be chosen to receive the nimble F-16 Fighting Falcon. *(H. J. van Broekshuizen)*

Below: Although the F-4C was converted to the 'Wild Weasel' role it saw service alongside the F-105G rather than replacing it. However, with the decision to convert the F-4E to F-4G standard the Thud was eventually supplanted. The jets were the least tired of the breed and were passed to the Georgia ANG at Dobbins AFB, Atlanta, where along with the 'D's at Hill they saw out the last few years of the type's service. *(Peter R. Foster)*

Opposite: The 'G' models were based upon the twin seat 'F' batches. These were the last of the 833 Thuds produced and 63-8256 depicted here was within the last 100 off the Republic line. The nose markings, although popularly referred to as 'Sharks Mouth' were in fact Weasel Mouths and as such were only applied to the F-105G variant. *(Lindsay Peacock)*

Below: The first unit to become operational with the Dart was the 498thFIS at Geiger Field, Spokane, Washington. This unit was declared to NORAD in May 1959 but so fast was technology moving that in the following year the type was to receive 63 modifications to the control system and 67 to the airframe. This shot is of 58-0786 belonging to the 460thFIS at McChord AFB circa 1972.

Opposite: Of all the Century fighters the Convair F-106 Delta Dart was produced in the smallest numbers. Having said this, starting life as the F-102B, the aircraft was the only type designed for a specific role, which it served faithfully for nearly thirty years. The clean lines of this design are ably demonstrated in this shot of 57-2502 taken early in the type's introduction.

Below: Delays in the introduction of the Dart to operational service between the first flight in December 1956 and introduction in May 1959 were primarily caused by the service certification of the J-75 engine and bugs in the then revolutionary MA-1 fire control system. However, the airframe was to become the mainstay of the NORAD defence force, serving with regular and Air National Guard units alike. Here 59-0132 is seen in the markings of the 48thFIS stationed at Langley AFB. The unit patch portrayed an outline of a Dart with a Tazanglian Devil superimposed over the top whilst their motto includes the legend 'Protectors of TAC'.

Opposite: One of the major modifications to be incorporated in the F-106 was the introduction of an inflight refuelling capability. Therefore since 1967 the aircraft has been deployed to Korea, Labrador and Germany on air defence duties. The deployment to Germany occurred in 1975 when the 5thFIS from Minot AFB detached six aeroplanes to Bitburg AFB during the annual 'Crested Cap' deployment. This was the only occasion in recent times when the Dart visited European shores. Here clustered around a KC-135A a pair of 48FIS F-106s take on fuel to increase their CAP time.

Below: The regular F-106 units also maintained 'alert' facilities and in this shot an aircraft from the 49thFIS at Griffiths AFB can be seen landing with the alert barns in the background. The regular F-106 units also held detached alert stations which in all cases, with the exception of the 49th, were in the southern states' warmer climes. The 49th held its 'remote' at Loring AFB in northern Maine during the late seventies, having moved from its previous location at New Hanover County Airport, North Carolina. (Peter R. Foster)

Opposite: By the mid-seventies the venerable Dart was serving with no less than six Air National Guard units, all of which were assigned to NORAD. These units held regular 'alert' facilities in common with their regular airforce counterparts. The units also deployed for regular air combat training and live missile firing exercises alongside other NORAD assigned units. Here a gleaming Dart from the 191stFIS at Selfridge ANGB is seen at Williams AFB, Arizona. (Peter R. Foster)

Below: The demise of the 'Dart' began in earnest by the beginning of the eighties. In the mid-seventies, apart from the six ANG units, NORAD still maintained six regular F-106 squadrons which consisted of 5thFIS at Minot, 48thFIS at Langley, 49thFIS at Griffiths, 84thFIS at Castle as depicted here, 87thFIS at K. I. Sawyer and 318thFIS at McChord.
(Peter R. Foster)

Opposite: Weapons training was primarily conducted from Tyndall AFB in Florida where once every two years the 'William Tell' air to air weapons meet was held. The meet, in NORAD days, was as much a social event as a competition. This led to some interesting variations to aircraft colour schemes whilst the overall condition of the jets would do justice to any proud owner. In 1980 when this shot was taken the F-106 category was won by the 144thFIW California ANG but the 49thFIS took that trophy in the 1978 and 1982 events.
(Peter R. Foster)

Below: Only three regular F-106 units were to convert to the mighty F-15 Eagle. These were the 5th, 48th and 318th FIS. However as plans stand at present these are scheduled to deactivate, passing the F-15s onto the Air National Guard which will result in the entire NORAD air defence fighter chain being run by the National Guard. The first to stand down was the 5th FIS at Minot which passed its 'Eagles' onto the Massachusetts ANG at Otis ANGB in 1988. Here just beginning to rotate are a pair of 318th Darts. *(Peter R. Foster)*

Opposite: 'Fighter Afil' is pre-planned training with aircraft of differing types from units who gain mutual training from such engagements. The F-106 having a prime role of bomber interceptor therefore undertook regular sorties against the mighty B-52 of SAC. Here clustered around B52G 58-0210 are a quartet of 'Darts' from the New Jersey ANG. *(Don Spering/AIR)*

Below: Seen over its home town of Atlantic City, this F-106A, 59-0007, was one of the last of the type to remain in operational service. The 119thFIS 177FIG New Jersey ANG traded in the final Delta Darts during the summer of 1988 when it converted to the F-16 Fighting Falcon. *(Lindsay Peacock)*

Opposite: The 'dual' version of the Delta Dart came about at a very early stage in the aircraft's development, the air force and the company having learned the lessons of time. The F-106B was funded in three out of the four years of production contracts, giving an overall split of 277 single seat and 63 twin seat aircraft. Here landing at McGuire AFB with chute streaming and air brakes out is 59-0149 the first F-106B of the final production batch in the colours of the 177FIG New Jersey ANG. *(Peter R. Foster)*

Right: The prime weapon employed by the F-106 was the Falcon missile in either the AIM-4A or AIM-26B versions, the latter being the Nuclear Falcon. In the types' twilight years, development on the introduction of a 20mm Vulcan cannon and 'snap shot' gunsight gained momentum but this really came too late to be of significant use. But even with missile capability alone, an altitude limit in excess of 57,000 feet and a speed of at least Mach 1.9 together with a Delta wing made it no mean performer. Here seen at altitude over southern central Canada is 57-2496 of the Montana ANG or 'Big Sky Country'. *(Don Jay)*

Far right: Humour has been a very important part of the 'William Tell' meet over the past few decades and the engine exhaust cover of this 186thFIS Montana ANG F-106A was no exception. In fact during the 1982 meet the entire detachment received art work which were variations on this theme. *(Peter R. Foster)*

Below: Apart from the front line and guard units that were to operate the F-106, the Air Defence Weapons Centre was to be the major user of the type. Located at Tyndall as the F-106 training unit and weapon instructor unit the 95FITS working alongside the Voodoos of 2FITS and T-33As of 65FITS provided the bulk of pilots in the NORAD world. Similarly during such events as 'William Tell' the unit was charged with providing some of the targets for the various profiles. Here seen cleaning up is F-106B 57-2536 in the final markings of the ADWC during the autumn of 1980.
(Peter R. Foster)

Opposite: Montana was part of the final quartet of Dart Squadrons. At that time in the mid-eighties the final two regular units of 49th and 87thFIS were about to deactivate completely whilst both Montana and New Jersey were to convert to the F-16. Montana had completed its changeover to the Fighting Falcon by the beginning of 1988 and now maintains its alert facility with that type, employing an almost identical scheme to that used on the F-106. Here taxiing past a line of PQM-102 and QF-100 drone aircraft is 57-2487 during the 1982 'William Tell' competition.
(Peter R. Foster)

Below: Bright markings were always the order of the day while NORAD came under the command of ADC. However with the transfer to TAC in the early eighties this was very much frowned upon. This was clearly evident at the subsequent 'William Tell' meets during which it was not considered 'professional' to indulge in such a way! Here with one of the brightest markings in latter years is 59-0105 of 5thFIS seen at McChord AFB. *(Doug Remington)*

Opposite: The first 'Guard' Dart unit to stand down in favour of the F-16 was 159thFIS Florida ANG which converted to the Fighting Falcon in early 1987. Here over the eastern seaboard is F-106A 58-0784 displaying the unit's distinctive markings. The code '21' on the rear fuselage belies the fact that the unit's three or four T-33As were included in the coding system. The unit was originally housed at Imeson Airport in Jacksonville but moved to a new facility at Jacksonville International in the early seventies. The unit now holds an alert detachment at Homestead AFB south of Miami. *(H. J. van Broekshuizen)*

Below: Although there were many units to operate the F-106 some merely changed identity as politics dictated. For instance the 11thFIS at K. I. Sawyer eventually became the 87thFIS. The markings between these two units were, in 1962, red and white stripes on the tail with a blue chevron. By 1969 this had altered to a large red delta outlined in black and in its final form this was altered to a red bulls head reflecting with the unit's nickname.

Overleaf: Across a shimmering sea this F-106 puts on the 'g' to bring the target to bear. However the Dart was never to see action, unlike so many other American types and all of the other Century Series fighters. It was however to intercept more Russian aircraft than all the others with the exception of the FMS F-104s. The prime trade of the NORAD units is transiting Russian Tu-144 Bears en route to and from Cuba. *(Lindsay Peacock)*

Opposite: A characteristic of the Dart was the clam shell air brakes at the rear of the square vertical fin. Also housed here was the brake parachute. The jet depicted here, 59-0031, belongs to the 177FIG New Jersey ANG and is about to touch down at McGuire AFB during the October of 1981. *(Peter R. Foster)*

Below: The United States Bicentennial celebrations were an open licence for units to go overboard with outlandish paint schemes with almost anything being considered acceptable. This 318thFIS example was tame compared to some designs to emerge during this exotic period. *(Don Jay)*

Opposite: Perhaps one of the most tasteful designs for the 1776-1976 celebrations was that applied by the 49thFIS. Using some initiative they adapted the serial of 59-0076 to read 17 900 76 on the port side and 19 900 76 on the starboard.

Below: Although there seemed at one time little likelihood of the Dart entering the world of controlled drones there was at least one airframe to remain airworthy in 1990. This is F-106B 57-2507 which as N607NA operated with NASA from both the Langley and Cleveland facilities. How long this will survive is anyone's guess but with in excess of 160 different spares sources available at Davis Monthan it could conceivably continue until the next century. *(Don Jay)*

Opposite: From one extreme to another, the most outlandish scheme must have been on 58-0760 of the Florida ANG. Once again an aeroplane with '76' in its serial presentation was used. The resulting paint scheme, suitably inscribed 'City of Jacksonville', says the rest. *(Don Jay)*

Below: 59-0128 of the 48thFIS breaks away.